Watch Me Make a Birthday Card

By Jack Otten

Welcome Books

Children's Press®
A Division of Scholastic Inc.
New York / Toronto / London / Auckland / Sydney
Mexico City / New Delhi / Hong Kong

Photo Credits: Cover and all photos by Maura Boruchow
Contributing Editor: Jennifer Silate
Book Design: Michelle Innes

Library of Congress Cataloging-in-Publication Data

Otten, Jack.
Watch me make a birthday card / by Jack Otten.
    p. cm. -- (Making things)
Includes index.
Summary: Provides step-by-step instructions for making a birthday card.
ISBN 0-516-23948-1 (lib. bdg.) -- ISBN 0-516-23498-6 (pbk.)
1. Greeting cards--Juvenile literature. [1. Greeting cards. 2. Birthdays. 3. Handicraft.] I. Title.

TT872 .O88 2002
745.594'1--dc21

                                        2001042362

Contents

My name is Maggie.

Tomorrow is my friend Jane's birthday.

I am going to make a **birthday card** for her.

5

I will use yellow paper.

I will also use colored **markers**.

First, I fold the paper in **half**.

9

Then, I write Jane's name on the front.

I **draw** stars on the birthday card.

I use the blue marker to draw the stars.

13

I also draw hearts on the front.

I use the red marker to draw the hearts.

On the inside of the card,
I write "Happy Birthday."

I write my name on the inside, too.

Now, Jane will know that the card is from me.

Jane's birthday card is finished.

I cannot wait to give it to her!

21

New Words

birthday card (**burth**-day **kard**) a paper note that has happy birthday wishes written on it

draw (**draw**) to make a picture of something with a pen, pencil, or marker

half (**haf**) one of two equal parts that together make a whole

markers (**mar**-kuhrs) large pens with colored ink

To Find Out More

Books

Kids Create!: Art & Craft Experiences for 3- to 9-Year-Olds
by Laurie Carlson
Williamson Publishing

The Big Book of Cool Crafts: Playing with Paint, Paper, and Models
by Sara Lynn
The Lerner Publishing Group

Web Site
EnchantedLearning.com's Card Crafts
http://www.enchantedlearning.com/crafts/cards/index.shtml
This site has many fun card-making projects for kids.

Index

About the Author
Jack Otten is an author and educator living in New York City.

Reading Consultants
Kris Flynn, Coordinator, Small School District Literacy, The San Diego County Office of Education

Shelly Forys, Certified Reading Recovery Specialist, W.J. Zahnow Elementary School, Waterloo, IL

Sue McAdams, Former President of the North Texas Reading Council of the IRA, and Early Literacy Consultant, Dallas, TX